ME, MY FEELINGS AND I

Life experiences, Lessons, Motivation

Palak Thakkar

BookLeaf Publishing

India | USA | UK

Made with ❤ on the BookLeaf Publishing Platform
www.bookleafpub.in
www.bookleafpub.com

Dedication

To my mother, who always believed in me;
To my grandmother, who always encouraged me;
To my bestie, who always has been there for me;
To my sister, who encouraged me;
And to the people who gave me so many lessons —
With every heartbreak, I learned something, and I turned
my pain into creativity, with a hope that someone who
relates will not feel alone, and to inspire them to choose
to be kind and be true to themselves even in their tough
times, and always be who they are.

Preface

I chose to step into the world of words where creativity is our priority and inspiring and sharing stories makes us happy. I chose to write this book to share my experiences, my lessons, and to inspire others.
I hope people can understand that being kind means sticking to being human, and it helps us make this world a better place to live in.
I believe and hope that people can help each other and be there for the ones in need. All it takes is a feeling to help to get a change.
I hope my book inspires one to be kind and become a better version of them.

Acknowledgements

Thanks to everyone who entered my life, because I believe we all meet for a reason — where some people come into our lives to teach us lessons, while some come into our lives to help us stand strong in our tough times. I always believed, and I still do believe, in "farista," which in English means an "angel."
I really am thankful to many people, but I will first thank my first farista — that's my Mom, Dr. Sonal. I have learned a lot from you, and I choose to walk in your footprints. Watching you handle your battles in a graceful way, I learned to be kind in the toughest times and to never give up, no matter what. You taught me to help others and to be who I am.
Mom, you always saw me with your perfect eyes, where the imperfect me, with so many flaws, was still beautiful in your eyes. You are my role model, and I feel blessed to be your daughter. Thanks for making me who I am today — you are the best Mom.

I am thankful to my Grandmother and Grandfather (my Nani and Nana) for supporting me to reach my goals and for always encouraging me to do my best in life. Watching them, I learned how to never give up and to stand strong when life throws challenges. With their love and care, I felt safe and secure.

I am so thankful to my Bestie — thanks for always being there and never leaving me. You have always believed in me and loved me not just as a bestie, but as a real sister. When my mind used to question me, your love made me feel so special and calmed me. It made me realize I am lovable, and that means a lot to me.

Thanks to my Sister, who encouraged me to write and submit my poems, and made me feel confident about them. Your support made me happy, and I felt secure knowing I have you — and that's what I need.

I am grateful to my Brothers for supporting me, making me smile in my tough times, and silently being there during my hardest times. I owe you people a lot. I hope nazar na lage because you all mean a lot.

Thanks a lot to my masis for being there, always understanding me, and supporting me.

I am thankful to the people whom I recently met. I felt a good change, and indirectly, unknowingly, they actually helped me — by being part of my healing. By spending time, I felt great.

I am thankful to God for guiding me always.

I thank my Close Ones for being there and taking care of
me.

Last but not least, I thank the ones who broke my heart
into pieces. Because while fixing myself, I found my
light, my purpose. I learned to let go and focused on self-
love. These lessons have helped me embrace myself and
brought out a better version of me.

It has quite been a journey — from never being a book
person to writing a book of poems.

1. I Feel Lonely

I feel lonely.
I am tired of hearing no's.
I keep on asking people to meet,
Just to hear their no's.
I don't know if it's an excuse or if they're actually busy,
Because once they have time, they never ask me to join.
I live in a world of hope,
Where I get the attention I deserve,
The love I crave,
And the care I desire.
Hoping someday I will find my people,
Who will understand me without me saying that I need them.
Hoping someday I will be their Plan A, not Plan B.

2. I Know I Am Just an Option

I'll be as far as you want me to go,
But the day you want me—
I'll be there, no matter where you go.

Time changes,
But I won't.
People leave,
But I won't.

I can't take your pain,
But I can be the reason you smile.

I might not be physically strong,
But still, I'll be your shield to protect you.
I will be the light in your darkest days,
The hope in your unwanted days.

My presence will bring calmness to your life,
As I will be the key to your lock.

I will fly away,
So will the problem.
Because once my job is done,
I know—I am just an option.

3. Fading Away from Your Life

Whenever you treat me as an option,
You choose to lose me.
Because little by little, every time,
It reminds me that I am just an option.

If I don't make an effort,
There's no chance of creating memories.
But someday, I will stop—
And you'll be left with only memories.

Relationships are stronger
When they're wanted by both sides.
You're happy without my presence,
And that made me realize
That fading away from your life
Is my only option.

4. It Will Take Me a While to Understand

It will take me a while to understand me better,
To know who I am,
What I want to chase later,
To know what I feel,
What I don't like any longer.
It will take me a while to understand me better.

5. Too Much to Let Go

I looked in the mirror—
It was someone who looked like me,
But not the same as who I was.

I smiled, but I wasn't happy.
I cried for the broken heart that I have,
Trying to build it piece by piece.

There are thoughts running through my head.
I feel like I'm stuck.
Don't know what's next.
There's so much in my head.

How do I breathe?
I feel heavy deep down.
I want to let go,
But I can't lose the hold—
It's too much to let go.

6. The Lesson I Learned

I might talk a lot, but will not say what is in my heart
because
I will smile all day with a broken heart and won't shed a
tear, no matter how badly I'm falling apart.
I stopped expressing myself, expecting,
The day I realised I was never chosen, no matter how
much I say.
I always gave so much of me—
Little did I know, it was always about them and never
about me.
Temporary need of mine
Was something they needed.
Support, hope, a shoulder, healer—were only needed.
Little misunderstanding I had, all the misconceptions
cleared
The day I realised my relationship was never needed.

7. I Have Started Changing Myself

I have started changing me.
Even if I feel like meeting people,
I have stopped asking them to meet me.
I have expectations,
But I tell myself,
Reality is different,
And no one likes to spend time with me.
I wish people could see the love I have for them—
How I want to cherish them.
Every memory, I want to capture with them.
But I tell myself,
Do not expect.
Do not remind them.
Do not ask them.
Let them decide.
If they want me in their life, they will try again.

8. HOPE IS MY ONLY OPTION

My heart feels heavy with emotions.
My mind is having multiple thoughts.
I'm fighting to smile.
Surviving today is my job.
Tears in my eyes,
Smile on my face.
Hiding what I feel,
Because no one cares.
Someday someone I will find,
Who will care.
Hiding won't be an option,
Because they will understand me.
Having hope right now is my only option.

9. I Need to Correct Myself

I need to correct me.
My vision seems to be blurry.
They can't see what my heart wants to see—
Because they are too scared to face reality,
Too afraid to accept everything was nothing but an
expectation.

I need to correct me.
My heart aches every day.
My eyes shed too much unspoken pain in the form of
tears.
But still, my heart loves those who made it ache.
My eyes still wish to see them stay beside me—
The same ones who made me shed those tears.

I need to correct me.
I'm losing me.
I'm fading every day
Just to make them want me,

Just to make them stay.

They all see it.
They notice and do nothing.
Or maybe they're too busy to notice—or to care.

I need to correct me.
Even after explaining, I am not understood.
Even after the puffy eyes and red nose,
The situation is not understood.

Maybe I'm not that important to anyone.
Maybe I'm just not made for anyone.

It's okay.
I need to correct myself
By learning to choose me.

10. Oh No, Anxiety

Oh no, anxiety,
You made me lose control.
You shook me from inside
And made me think of the worst.
My chest got tight,
I couldn't breathe,
Felt too much.

I told myself, "Someday I will be fine."
Today I have to bear, but tomorrow I will be fine.
This battle, I'm not losing.
I will fight until the day I am winning,
Where I regain control of my life,
Where I can live every moment stress-free and not panic
about what will happen next.
Where I don't depend on pills, nor I will ever need them,
And realize I am far better than I was in the past.

11. Goodbyes Are Just Words

Some goodbyes are just by words.
We are connected by heart.
We don't hold hands anymore—
We hold on to memories.
We are not forever,
But we were the best in the temporary.
The mind will remember the words,
The heart will remember the feelings.
My actions will prove my love—
Filled with care, effort, and kindness they used to be.
Things ended,
But I still feel the same.
You moved on,
But I still feel the same.
I became a hero in your story by letting you go.
You became a villain in my story for asking to let go.
It was not just the bond that ended—
My trust, hope, and expectations,
They all ended.

Even if we are not together,
I can't hold on to you,
And things ended forever.
I will cherish the memories
And hold on to them forever.

12. MY SECRET HERO

You are my secret hero.
You brought my lost smile back.
You fixed the broken version of me.
You gave me the opportunity to rise back.
You were the mirror who never judged me.
You were the shield who protected me.
You were the superhero I needed—
that God gave me.

13. I Choose to Learn

I am scared of everything,
But I still face it.
I choose to try.
I believe it's okay to fail.
It is good to learn,
And better to improve.

14. Today I Am Drowning in Learning

Today I am drowning in pain,
Tomorrow I will hold myself again.
Pain isn't forever,
So let me dive in again.

I will shine brighter,
I will prove myself again.
Because today I am drowning to learn,
Tomorrow I will let the sparks of the
lesson—
And this time, let me hold myself again.

Let me hold others again,
Let me not let anyone drown again.

15. I Learned to Be There for Myself

While being there for others, I learned to be there for me.
While helping people,
I learned to help me.
While making others smile,
I learned to smile by myself.
While being there for others, I learned to be there for me.

16. Let Me Rewrite the Story

Dwelling in the past
Is sorting nothing.
Overthinking is sorting out nothing.
So let me live in the moment.
Let me focus on the present.
This will create a better future.
I am the creator of my own life.
Let me rewrite the story.
Let me make some changes.
Let me bring back me by a loud comeback.
Let me walk the road of success and make a comeback.

17. New Journey of Mine

Each step I walk through
Is a learning phase of mine.
Changing chapters with new characters
Is a new journey of mine.

I am scared to enter a new chapter,
But I am brave enough to start one.

18. Saying "Hi" to Me Again

Saying goodbye to you,
So I say hi to me again.
I am letting you go,
To hold myself again.
I stopped crying,
To smile again.
I am walking with the flow,
To learn to ride life again.

19. I Found Me

Even after losing you, I won.
I lost you, but I found me.
Those broken pieces of me—
I gathered them and fixed me.

My chapter in your life ends,
And I flip the tables.
When I started writing my own story,
I healed me.

You are you, and I am me.
That's the difference
Between you and me.
You chose others over me—
But this time, I chose me.

Self-love is a journey I walk onto.
Embracing myself, by myself,
Is the lesson I learned.

Because even after losing you, I won.
I lost you, but I found me.

20. I Saved Me

Pain hit me hard
The day I lost me.
I changed my mindset to embrace me.
The journey was tough,
But I didn't leave me.

The craving for care, love, and attention I wanted—
I gave me.
I didn't have people,
But I had me.

I always reminded this to myself:
I was my healer and a hero.
And that's what I needed
To save me.

21. WHO I AM

I no more need validation.
I am who I am.
I don't need to explain.
I am who I am.
I am not changing me to fit in people's lives.
I will be me and do the best in one's life.
I am powerful, I am kind.
I am learning, growing, and ready to shine.
I stand for me to respect me.
I clap for me to appreciate me.
I am doing things for myself and I.
I'm learning to become who I am.

22. Don't Take Me for Granted

Don't ignore me.
You will miss my efforts,
Even when I will be beside you.
You will not have the same me.
I will not sacrifice my self-respect,
So don't take me for granted.

I am being kind and sweet—
I am not running behind you.
Even I deserve the same amount of effort
Which I give you.
So please don't ignore me.

23. You Are the Change

Be wise with your words.
Be kind with your actions.
A person like you is rare—
Shouldn't be treated as an option.

Don't let people change you,
When you're the change.
Let the world make the noise,
But you dance to the beat of your heart.

No matter how dark the days are,
You will still shine bright—
As bright as your kind heart.

24. I Believe in the Moment Now

I am enjoying life.
I am doing far better than yesterday.
I wake up feeling happy and blessed.
I am excited for the day.
I feel low sometimes,
But I am happy again the other time.

I am grateful for the ones
Who helped me change.
Unknowingly, they helped me heal.
They were the reason I learned to feel again.
They made me smile at my new chapter,
Changed my perspective towards life for the better.

I believe in the moment now.
I will cherish this forever.

25. I Am Living in the Moment

I don't know what will happen tomorrow,
But for the first time, I'm living in the moment.
It's so special to feel this way,
Where what I feel now matters more.

My mind is calm.
I smile more.
I wake up with peace.
I sleep with excitement about the upcoming day.

I don't know what will happen tomorrow,
But I will enjoy each moment today.
I will treasure today.
I will create a lot of good memories today.

26. Chasing Life Like a Dreamer

Chasing life like a dreamer is my dream,
Flying high with my wings.

I may have failed when I walked the stairs of success,
But I didn't give up—because I knew the reason why I
started.

Today is my opportunity to make tomorrow better.
This is the reason why I started to walk on the road of
my dream:
To make one's life better.

27. Building a Home of Dreams

Building a career
Is like building a home of dreams,
Where there's no limit to flying high,
Where there's no chance to lose hope—until you rise
high.

Growth is a journey,
Where steps are the failures.
Each lesson is a medal of survival and learning.
Without passing these,
There's no chance to rise high.

28. Dear Life

Dear life, let's live again.
Let's forget what we've been through and try again.
It's not easy, but it's not impossible.
Changes are okay; let's make this possible.
Today is an opportunity; let's grab it.
Let's make tomorrow better and rewrite the chapter.
Let's not forget who we are,
And rock on to the next chapter.

29. My Kindness Didn't Shake

Because I have been sick,
Days have passed,
Nights feel the same.
People pass by,
And the dates change—
But why the hell am I still the same?

Everything happened,
But I didn't change.
I wasn't ready for this chapter.
You came and broke me,
Yet still, I slayed.

My happiness was gone,
But my kindness didn't shake.
And maybe this is who I am—
And it's good nothing has changed.

30. We Are Humans

We are humans,
So let's act like one.
Be kind, have humanity, and forgive one another.

We all make mistakes—
We all are learners.
We all are in pain—
And we all need a healer.

Let us heal,
Let us understand each other.
Let's make this world a better place,
And be kind to each other.

31. Dear Diary

People will come and go,
They will teach you before they go.
Don't worry about who stays or leaves—
Don't allow yourself to leave you.

These days are never coming back.
Dear Diary, these people I met—
I will never leave them back.

People come and go,
But these people made a home in my heart.
Even if they leave me,
I will always cherish them in my heart.

32. Bond of Friendship

I just met you,
You made my life better.
Things changed for the better—
God sent the person you are.

I hope you don't change,
And always stay the same as you are.
I hope you don't break my heart.
All I ask for is honesty and loyalty
From the bottom of your heart.

Last but not least,
I hope our bond of friendship
Is never judged.

33. You Are My World

I may be asking for too much,
But I do—because you mean too much.
I wish I was as important in your life
As you are in mine.

I wish you could see the change in me around you,
To know how your presence makes my day.
Maybe I can't digitally capture all the memories,
But they are surely deeply captured by the heart.

I wish my words could do justice to my emotions,
As there's a lot to say—but I lack the words.
My world revolves around you,
And you are my world.

34. You Are the Reason I Believe In Forever

You were my shield.
You are my mirror.
You never judged me.
You are my forever.

You are the reason for my smile.
You are the fire brigade of my life.
You are my healer.
You are my pride.

I can never forget what you did for me.
You always put me first,
No matter what I do,
Where I go.

I will hold on to you,
Wherever I go.
This bond is forever.
You are the reason

I believe in forever.

35. Holding Onto Yourself is a Priority

At the beginning of life,
When we start learning,
One of the first things we learn is to hold.
We hold onto people,
We hold onto memories.
But when the time comes,
We fall, get up, and learn to hold on to ourselves.
Life teaches us this continuously in every chapter—
That holding on to others can be an option,
But holding yourself should always be a priority.
People come and go,
Things start and end.
What walks with us till the end is we ourselves.
When we learn to hold on to ourselves,
We cry, we wipe our tears.
We take a stand for ourselves.
We become better,
And that's how we grow.

36. I Am Rare

I don't leave people.
They leave me.
So I can only say,
I will be the best temporary person in your life.
Yet still, you will replace me,
But will never feel what I made you feel again.
I am rare, and you didn't realize this.
You just didn't choose to lose me,
But you chose to lose a diamond like me.

37. See Things from Someone Else's Perspective

Be grateful for what you have.
You want a lot more,
But enough you have.

Someone's dream car you drive,
Someone's dream job you have.
You are running the business of one's dream.
You have good mental and physical health.

You sleep under a roof which you call home.
You eat what you want—
You even order your meals one can't afford.
You live the life one prays for.

Someone's dream is to be like you.
Someone admires your beauty.
Someone craves the love and attention you get.
Someone prays to get the parents and family you have.
Someone prays to live a life like yours.

Be grateful for what you have.
See from others' perspective the life you have had.

38. I Dream of Being Rich Enough

I dream to be rich enough
Where I feed the needy ones food,
Where somebody I could pay for the bill of hospital.
I could be the reason one smile,
I could give a hand to help them in their bad time.
I want to be rich enough to save one's life.
I want to make the life of people better.
If I could be rich enough to make one's wish come true.

39.

The Healer Everyone Needed

I am the unwanted, yet the most needed person—
Not a priority, for sure, just an option.
Not invited on happy days,
But always called on the sad days.

I'm tagged by the name of friend and sister,
But treated like an option.
I wipe their pain;
In return, they give me pain.

I make their hearts smile,
But I'm the one left crying.
I'm a fixer of broken hearts,
But I've been broken by most of the hearts.

40. Just Give Me a Chance

I know you are scared of heartbreaks,
But allow me to stay.
I will heal the broken you
And help you slay.

Your fears will say goodbye,
Happiness will say hi to you.
Just give me a chance,
I will make it up to you.

Tell me your story,
I will listen and not judge.
I will help you stand again,
I will be your backbone.

I won't let you down,
Just give me a chance—
I will make it up to you.

www.ingramcontent.com/pod-product-compliance
Lightning Source LLC
LaVergne TN
LVHW010020200726

843495LV00015B/1851

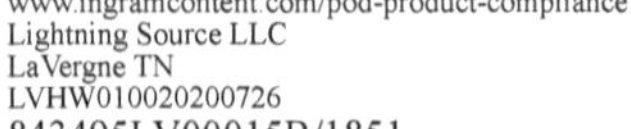